Religious Celebrations

Ian Rohr

Smart Apple Media
P.O. Box 3263
Mankato, MN, 56002

First published in 2010 by
MACMILLAN EDUCATION AUSTRALIA PTY LTD
15–19 Claremont St, South Yarra, Australia 3141

Visit our web site at www.macmillan.com.au or go directly to www.macmillanlibrary.com.au

Associated companies and representatives throughout the world.

Library of Congress Cataloging-in-Publication Data

Rohr, Ian.
    Religious celebrations / Ian Rohr.
        p. cm. -- (Celebrations around the world)
    Includes index.
    ISBN 978-1-59920-539-7 (library binding)
    1. Fasts and feasts--Juvenile literature. 2. Festivals--Juvenile literature. I. Title.
    BL590.R65 2011
    203'.6--dc22
                                2009042144

Publisher: Carmel Heron
Managing Editor: Vanessa Lanaway
Editor: Michaela Forster
Proofreader: Kirstie Innes-Will
Designer: Kerri Wilson (cover and text)
Page layout: Pier Vido
Photo researcher: Wendy Duncan
Production Controller: Vanessa Johnson

Manufactured in China by Macmillan Production (Asia) Ltd.
Kwun Tong, Kowloon, Hong Kong
Supplier Code: CP January 2010

Acknowledgments
The author and the publisher are grateful to the following for permission to reproduce copyright material:

Cover photograph: South Korean Buddhist devotees praying on the Buddha's birthday, © Jung Yeon-Je/AFP/Getty Images

AAP Image/Charles Dharapak, 20; AAP Image/Bassem Tellawi, 21; AAP Image/Ed Wray, 8; © Kazuyoshi Nomachi/Corbis, 7; © Khalen El-Fiqi/Corbis, 19; © Made Nagi/epa/Corbis/epa, 24; © Ken Seet/Corbis, 26; © Paul Souders/Corbis, 25; © Dreamstime/Nikhil Gangavane, 27; © Jan Cook/Foodpix/Getty Images, 13; © Paul Chesley Getty Images, 6; © Gary Moss Photography/Getty Images, 17; © Nina Raingold Getty Images, 12; © Khin Maung Win/AFP/Getty Images, 23; © Jung Yeon-Je/AFP/Getty Images, 1, 22; © iStockphoto/Jeremy Edwards, 5; © iStockphoto/Sean Locke, 9; © iStockphoto/Jack Puccio, 15; © iStockphoto/Charles Shapiro, 16; photolibrary/Kindra Clineff, 4; photolibrary/Martin Harvey, 29; photolibrary/Photo Researchers, 14; photolibrary/Amit Somvanshi, 28; © Shutterstock/Mikhail Levit, 10; © Shutterstock/motorolka, 11; © Shutterstock/Vladimir Melnik, 18; © Shutterstock/Kevin Renes, 30.

While every care has been taken to trace and acknowledge copyright, the publisher tenders their apologies for any accidental infringement where copyright has proved untraceable. Where the attempt has been unsuccessful, the publisher welcomes information that would redress the situation.

Contents

When a word is printed in **bold**, you can look up its meaning in the Glossary on page 31.

Celebrations

Celebrations are events that are held on special occasions. Some are events from the past that are still celebrated. Others celebrate important times in our lives or activities, such as music.

Birthdays are special events that many people celebrate.

Some celebrations involve only a few people.
Others involve whole cities or countries.
Large celebrations take place across the world.

New Year's Eve is celebrated all around
the world with fireworks.

What Are Religious Celebrations?

Religious celebrations are times when important religious events are remembered. Some religious celebrations are held on the same day every year.

Followers of Islam pray in a place called a **mosque** during religious celebrations.

Some religious celebrations have changed over time. Other celebrations are new. However, most religious celebrations are hundreds of years old.

Many Buddhist celebrations have been passed down from many years ago.

Christmas, Christianity

Christmas is celebrated by Christians around the world. It celebrates the birth of Jesus. This was on December 25, which is known as Christmas Day.

Many Christians go to special church services on Christmas Eve and Christmas Day.

Christmas is a favorite celebration for many children. On Christmas Day, people are given presents. This is because three wise men gave presents to the baby Jesus.

People receive presents from their family and friends at Christmas.

Easter, Christianity

Easter is a Christian celebration. It celebrates the **rebirth** of Jesus after his death on the cross. The date of Easter changes each year, but it is always around March or April.

At Easter, Christians gather to celebrate Jesus coming back to life.

At Easter, children are given chocolate Easter eggs. The eggs represent new life. Many Christians attend church during Easter.

Eggs are sometimes decorated at Easter.

Day of the Dead, Christianity

The Day of the Dead is a **Latin American** festival. It takes place on November 1 and 2 each year. Christians remember friends and family who have died.

Christians visit the graves of loved ones during the festival.

A Day of the Dead **tradition** is making **altars**, which are decorated with flowers. The favorite food and drink of the dead person are also put on the altars.

Sugar skulls represent death and **rebirth** and are placed on altars during the festival.

Passover, Judaism

Passover is a Jewish festival held in March or April. It celebrates the saving of the Jewish people from slavery many years ago.

Jewish people gather together to pray and eat during Passover.

Special meals are eaten during Passover. Houses are cleaned, and forbidden foods such as cakes and cereal are removed. Families also search their homes for any crumbs.

Passover has strict rules about which foods can be eaten.

Hanukkah, Judaism

Hanukkah (say *ha-nook-kah*) is a Jewish celebration that lasts for eight days in November or December. Candles are lit to remember a great victory by the Jewish people.

Candles are lit in a special candleholder called a menorah.

Hanukkah is a popular celebration for children. Schools are closed and special foods are eaten. Children play with **dreidels**, and many receive presents.

The words on the dreidels help children remember the Hanukkah story.

Eid al-Adha, Islam

Eid al-Adha (say *eed-al-addar*) is a **Muslim** celebration held in November or December. It usually lasts for three days. It celebrates the end of a **pilgrimage** by the Muslim people.

Many Muslims go to mosques to pray during Eid al-Adha.

Sheep are killed and the meat is given to family, friends, and poor people. Children are given presents, and they eat special foods.

Eid al-Adha is celebrated with a large feast.

Eid al-Fitr, Islam

Eid al-Fitr (say *eed-al-fitter*) is a Muslim celebration held at the end of Ramadan. Ramadan is a month when people **fast** from sunrise to sunset. Eid al-Fitr is held in September or October.

Muslims wear special clothes and wave flowers to celebrate the end of Ramadan.

People celebrate the end of Ramadan with a large feast. They also decorate their homes. Eid al-Fitr is a time to forgive people for any wrong things they have done.

Eid al-Fitr is celebrated with a feast of special foods.

Buddha Day, Buddhism

Buddha Day, which is also known as Wesak (or Vesak), is an important Buddhist celebration. People remember the birth and death of Buddha.

Buddhists gather together at **temples** to celebrate Buddha Day.

Buddha Day is celebrated on the first full moon in May. Buddhists gather at temples to pray and sing. They also make **offerings** of flowers, candles, and **incense**.

Buddhists make offerings to Buddha to thank him for his teachings.

On Buddha Day, Buddhists try not to kill any living thing. They also set birds and animals free. This is to show the importance of freedom for all animals.

Thousands of birds are released on Buddha Day.

People only eat **vegetarian food** on Buddha Day. Homes are cleaned and decorated, and special lanterns are made.

Many Buddhists celebrate Buddha Day with colourful lanterns.

Diwali, Hinduism

Diwali is a Hindu festival held in October or November. It is also known as the Festival of Lights. Lighting candles and setting off fireworks are part of the celebrations.

Lighting candles is an important part of celebrating Diwali.

Diwali lasts for five days and is celebrated around the world. During Diwali, many people wear new clothes. They also share snacks and sweets with each other.

Colorful paper lanterns are part of the Diwali festival.

Holi, Hinduism

Holi is a Hindu festival held in the spring. It is also called the Festival of Colors. This is because people throw colored paint, powder, and water at each other.

Many Hindus wear white clothes when throwing paint and water during Holi.

Holi celebrates spring and a very old Hindu **legend**. Large bonfires are lit and food is roasted on the fires. There is also singing and dancing.

During Holi, bonfires are lit to drive away bad spirits.

Try This!

Try This Quiz

Find the answers to these questions in the book.
(You can check your answers on page 32.)

1 Which religion celebrates Hanukkah?

2 Where is the Day of the Dead celebrated?

3 When is Eid al-Fitr celebrated?

4 What are released on Buddha Day?

5 What do people throw at each other during Holi?

Try This Activity

Next time you celebrate a special occasion with your friends or family, ask yourself:

• Why are you celebrating?

• How long have people been celebrating this event?

• Are there other places in the world where people celebrate the event?

Glossary

altars	special tables where offerings are made
dreidels	four-sided tops or toys
fast	a time when food is not eaten
incense	scented wood that smells nice when it burns
Latin American	from the countries and cultures of Central and South America and the Caribbean Islands
legend	a story from long ago
mosque	special building where Muslims go to worship
Muslim	a follower of the religion Islam
offerings	gifts to a god
pilgrimage	a religious journey to a special place
rebirth	coming back to life
temples	special buildings used for religious reasons
tradition	an activity or belief handed down from older people to younger people
vegetarian food	food that contains no meat

Index

Answers to the Quiz on Page 30

1 Judaism
2 Latin America
3 At the end of Ramadan, in September
   or October
4 Birds and animals
5 Colored paint, powder, and water